Thanks, Frank!

BROMLEY SWITZER | VIRVE ALJAS-SWITZER

ILLUSTRATIONS BY ROBERT ASKEW

EAST YORK PRESS

To our beloved furry friends,
both past and present—
you'll never be forgotten.

Sleepy Saturday mornings, hard to leave a cozy bed.

Who gives me extra snuggles?

Thanks, Frank!

Chilly toes in the morning air!

Who brings me
my slippers?

Thanks, Frank!

Starting our day with a walk to the park.

Who picks up the pace?

Thanks, Frank!

We love big breakfasts but not the cleanup.

Who helps us with the dishes?

Thanks, Frank!

Piles of dirty clothes that need washing.

Who helps sort the laundry?

Thanks, Frank!

Weekends are full of errands to run.

Who reminds me to enjoy the ride?

Thanks, Frank!

Bubbles help us get clean after a day of fun!

Who makes sure we all get a bath?

Thanks, Frank!

Family dinners bring us all together.

Who makes sure there are no leftovers?

Thanks, Frank!

Unwinding together with our favourite shows.

Who relaxed a little too much?

Thanks, Frank!

Furry cuddles before a busy week.

Who brings me sweet dreams?

Thanks, Frank!

The Real Frank

Frank is a real and very sweet dog that lives in Toronto
with his mom, Bromley. His favourite things are
playing fetch, swimming & his family—usually in that order.

9 781990 111100